Go Outside!
GO TO THE PARK!

By Peter Finn

Gareth Stevens
PUBLISHING

Please visit our website, www.garethstevens.com. For a free color catalog of all our high-quality books, call toll free 1-800-542-2595 or fax 1-877-542-2596.

Library of Congress Cataloging-in-Publication Data

Names: Finn, Peter, 1978- author.
Title: Go to the park! / Peter Finn.
Description: New York : Gareth Stevens Publishing, [2020] | Series: Go outside! | Includes index.
Identifiers: LCCN 2019009910| ISBN 9781538244937 (paperback) | ISBN 9781538244951 (library bound) | ISBN 9781538244944 (6 pack)
Subjects: LCSH: Parks–Juvenile literature.
Classification: LCC SB481.3 .F56 2020 | DDC 363.6/8–dc23
LC record available at https://lccn.loc.gov/2019009910

Published in 2020 by
Gareth Stevens Publishing
111 East 14th Street, Suite 349
New York, NY 10003

Copyright © 2020 Gareth Stevens Publishing

Editor: Therese Shea
Designer: Sarah Liddell

Photo credits: Cover, p. 1 Robert Kneschke/Shutterstock.com; p. 5 Tetyana Kaganska/Shutterstock.com; p. 7 barbsimages/Shutterstock.com; pp. 9, 24 (playground) Trong Nguyen/Shutterstock.com; p. 11 Hurst Photo/ Shutterstock.com; p. 13 wavebreakmedia/Shutterstock.com; p. 15 Jaycee3663/Shutterstock.com; pp. 17, 24 (garden) Konstanttin/Shutterstock.com; p. 19 Fishman64/Shutterstock.com; pp. 21, 24 (lawn) FreshStudio/ Shutterstock.com; p. 23 Sergey Novikov/Shutterstock.com.

Printed in the United States of America

Some of the images in this book illustrate individuals who are models. The depictions do not imply actual situations or events.

CPSIA compliance information: Batch #CW20GS: For further information contact Gareth Stevens, New York, New York at 1-800-542-2595.

Contents

My name is Pearl.
I love parks!

This is the city park.
I play soccer here.

This is the town park.
I go to the
playground here.

This is the state park.
I hike with my
cousins here.

This is a national park.
I camp with my
family here.

This is the dog park.
I bring my dog to
play here!

Some parks
have gardens.

Some parks
have woods.

Some parks have big green lawns. Let's have a picnic here!

I love parks!
Let's go to the park!

Words to Know

garden

lawn

playground

Index

24